Think Like a Scientist
DEVELOP AND TEST A HYPOTHESIS

Laura Loria

Britannica®
Educational Publishing

IN ASSOCIATION WITH

ROSEN
EDUCATIONAL SERVICES

Published in 2019 by Britannica Educational Publishing (a trademark of Encyclopædia Britannica, Inc.) in association with The Rosen Publishing Group, Inc.
29 East 21st Street, New York, NY 10010

Distributed exclusively by Rosen Publishing.
To see additional Britannica Educational Publishing titles, go to rosenpublishing.com.

First Edition

Britannica Educational Publishing
J.E. Luebering: Executive Director, Core Editorial
Mary Rose McCudden: Editor, Britannica Student Encyclopedia

Rosen Publishing
Amelie von Zumbusch: Editor
Nelson Sá: Art Director
Brian Garvey: Series Designer
Tahara Anderson: Book Layout
Cindy Reiman: Photography Manager
Karen Huang: Photo Researcher

Library of Congress Cataloging-in-Publication Data

Names: Loria, Laura, author.
Title: Develop and test a hypothesis / Laura Loria.
Description: New York : Britannica Educational Publishing, in Association with Rosen Educational Services, 2019 | Series: Think like a scientist | Audience: Grades 3—6. | Includes bibliographical references and index.
Identifiers: LCCN 2017048073| ISBN 9781538302422 (library bound) | ISBN 9781538302439 (pbk.) | ISBN 9781538302446 (6 pack)
Subjects: LCSH: Science—Methodology—Juvenile literature.
Classification: LCC Q175.2 .L67 2018 | DDC 507.2/1—dc23
LC record available at https://lccn.loc.gov/2017048073

Manufactured in the United States of America

Photo credits: Cover, p. 1 Jupiterimages/BananaStock/Thinkstock; cover (top), back cover, interior pages background cetus/Shutterstock.com; pp. 5, 21 Encyclopædia Britannica; p. 6 VW Pics/Universal Images Group/Getty Images; p. 7 Portra/DigitalVision/Getty Images; p. 8 Michael Nosek/Shutterstock.com; p. 9 Hero Images/Getty Images; p. 12 ESB Professional/Shutterstock.com; p. 13 Elena Nichizhenova/Shutterstock.com; p. 14 Photos.com/Thinkstock; pp. 16, 17 © National Library of Medicine; p. 18 Nathaniel Noir/Alamy Stock Photo; p. 20 Courtesy of the Rijksmuseum, Amsterdam, purchased with the support of the F.G. Waller-Fonds; p. 23 Steve Debenport/E+/Getty Images; p. 24 PeopleImages/E+/Getty Images; p. 26 Onfokus/E+/Getty Images; p. 28 Timofeev Vladimir/Shutterstock.com; p. 29 Lew Robertson/StockFood Creative/Getty Images.

CONTENTS

CHAPTER 1

INSIDE THE SCIENTIST'S MIND

How do things work in our universe? Why do they happen? People have always asked questions like these—especially scientists. Science is the search for knowledge about the universe and all that is in it.

Scientists look for natural explanations for things. For any problem they see, they try to understand the cause so they can come up with a solution. By learning what causes a disease, for example, scientists can work to control its spread.

THINK ABOUT IT

What are some ways that science has solved problems?

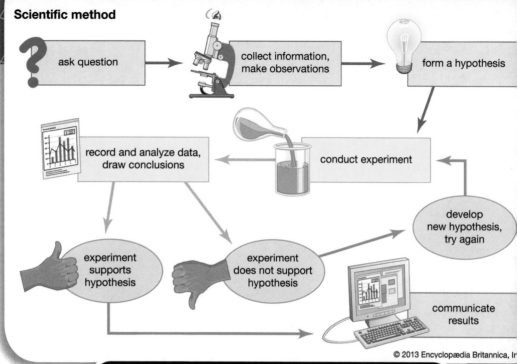

Scientific method

ask question

collect information, make observations

form a hypothesis

record and analyze data, draw conclusions

conduct experiment

experiment supports hypothesis

experiment does not support hypothesis

develop new hypothesis, try again

communicate results

© 2013 Encyclopædia Britannica, Ir

This diagram shows how scientists work through the scientific method.

To solve problems, scientists use something called the scientific method. They start by asking questions and finding out as much as possible about a topic or a problem. Then they make a hypothesis. A hypothesis is an attempt to explain a problem. They test the hypothesis with an **experiment**.

VOCABULARY

An **experiment** is the steps carried out to test a hypothesis.

5

If the experiment does not support the hypothesis, the scientists think about the problem again and develop a new hypothesis. They then test that hypothesis with a new experiment. If the experiment supports the hypothesis, other scientists repeat the experiment to make sure they get the same results. If they do get the same results, the hypothesis will be accepted as true until it can be proven false.

Scientists use the information they learn from testing many hypotheses to develop scientific

theories. A theory is a much broader explanation than a hypothesis. Scientists consider theories to be the best explanations for why certain things happen in the natural world. A theory may be changed if scientists discover new information about a topic.

Anyone can be a scientist. All you need is a curious mind, the willingness to ask a question and look for an answer, and some training. Using the scientific method is a way to satisfy your curiosity about the world around you.

CHAPTER 2

SMART GUESSES

Start with a question. Why does somethng happen the way it does? Think about it, read as much as you can about it, and ask other people what they think. Then make a hypothesis. A hypothesis is not a question. It is a statement, ending in a period. It's the answer that you guess will be

Many things that mystified people in the past, such as the appearance of rainbows, can be explained through science.

correct to your question, based on what you already know. After you make your hypothesis, then you do an experiment to test it.

When you write a hypothesis, choose strong, clear words. Instead of saying that something *might* be true, you say it *is* true. A hypothesis should sound very confident and direct. If your question asks *why*, the hypothesis should say *because*. A hypothesis is a guess, but it is a smart guess.

A question leads to a hypothesis. A hypothesis leads to predictions. In the scientific method, predictions are usually if/then statements. Let's say the question is "What will lead students to read more?" Your hypothesis might be, "Students will read more if they have a comfortable place to sit." The prediction might be, "If I put a couch in the reading area, then students will read for a longer period of time." Then you think about how you can test your prediction. That will be your experiment.

When testing a prediction, you must have a procedure, or a plan. You will also make a list of materials, the things you need to do the experiment. In this example, your procedure will be to record

COMPARE & CONTRAST

How is a prediction like a hypothesis? How is it different?

how long students read without the couch one week, and then record how long students read after the couch is brought in. Your material will be the couch. It is an independent **variable** in this experiment. An independent variable is the thing that a scientist changes on purpose to see what will happen. The students' reading time is the thing that you think will change in your experiment. That's called the dependent variable.Whenever possible, a scientist wants to control other variables. Maybe you would give students the same books to choose from each week of the experiment. This would ensure that the students' reading times don't change because

A scientist chooses her materials carefully, making sure she has everything she needs before she begins.

the books they choose are more or less interesting. Scientists can't control everything, though. This is why it's important to conduct many tests when doing an experiment.

Let's say that in your experiment you noticed an increase in how long students

THINK ABOUT IT

What are some factors that could affect an experiment?

In the couch experiment, the students are the subjects. Their behavior is what a scientist would track.

were reading after you gave them the couch. Then you might decide to test other hypotheses. You could provide students a snack, change the lighting in the room, or play music. These are other variables. You could test them to see if they changed students' reading habits. Once you have tested and proved several hypotheses, you could develop a scientific theory.

CHAPTER 3

PUTTING HYPOTHESES TO WORK

The scientific method has changed over time. For hundreds of years, people debated about the best way to conduct experiments. Teacher and philosopher Roger Bacon was an early supporter of what we now call the scientific method. He didn't make any big

Roger Bacon, who lived in the thirteenth century, was a priest and teacher at Oxford University in England.

discoveries of his own, but he believed that observation and experiment are the true basis of science.

People did not always know that **germs** can cause illness. We know it now because some scientists made observations, asked questions, and tested hypotheses about germs and illness. One of them was Dr. Ignaz Semmelweis. He noticed that the women who gave birth in his clinic were less likely to die if they were helped by a midwife, rather than a doctor or medical student.

VOCABULARY

Germs are tiny living things that can cause disease in plants or animals.

He wondered why this was so. He thought that maybe the doctors were carrying germs from the bodies they dissected in their training. The midwives would not have touched the bodies. His hypothesis was that germs from the bodies were transferred to the women having babies, causing their deaths.

Semmelweis proposed that if doctors washed their hands before delivering babies, the mothers would be less likely to die. When he ordered this at his clinic, the death rate went down. The same thing happened when he tried

Dr. Ignaz Semmelweis helped make medical procedures safer for patients through careful observation and testing of his hypothesis.

his experiment at another clinic. His hypothesis was correct, and now doctors are careful to wash their hands between patients.

Dr. John Snow also believed in germ theory, and he set out to prove it to the world. Snow lived in London in the first half of the nineteenth century. There were several outbreaks of cholera, a deadly infection of the intestine. At the time, people thought that cholera was spread through the air. Snow thought that the disease was spread through direct contact with feces, dirty water, and clothing. He had to prove his hypothesis that germs spread the disease by direct contact.

Dr. John Snow is also famous for developing safer ways to use anesthesia, medicine that helps people not feel pain during surgery.

The next cholera outbreak, in 1854, was Snow's chance to prove his hypothesis. He created graphs and maps tracking cholera infections. He found the source of the illness in a water pump on Broad Street in London. When he had the pump shut down, the number of illnesses fell. His next study, a larger one called "The Grand Experiment," also showed that dirty water was the cause of cholera infections. By proving his hypothesis about how people were getting cholera, Snow was also helping to prove germ theory. He is remembered as the father of epidemiology, the study of how diseases spread.

Charles Darwin was an English scientist who studied

A replica, or copy, of the pump that was determined to be the cause of a cholera outbreak was kept in Dr. Snow's memory until 2015.

How was Snow's experiment similar to Semmelweis's? How were they different?

nature. He is known for his theory of evolution by natural selection. According to this theory, all living things are struggling to survive. The living things that have the most helpful **traits** for their environ-ment tend to survive. For instance, an animal may have better vision or faster legs than other animals. These traits may help it find food and avoid its ene-mies. The animals with the helpful traits will be more likely to survive than ani-mals without those traits. When they reproduce they pass along their helpful traits to their young. Over

VOCABULARY

Traits are the special qualities of a living thing that make it what it is.

The theories of Charles Darwin shocked people at the time. They were debated for many years.

time, most of those animals will have that trait. In this way, plants and animals change, or evolve, over hundreds or thousands of years.

Darwin came up with his theory while on a five-year-long trip around the world. His goal was to study the natural history of the areas he visited. The observations Darwin made during the trip led him to wonder how new species developed. He proposed many hypotheses and performed experiments to test them. He described his ideas in his important book, *On the Origin of Species by Means of Natural Selection.*

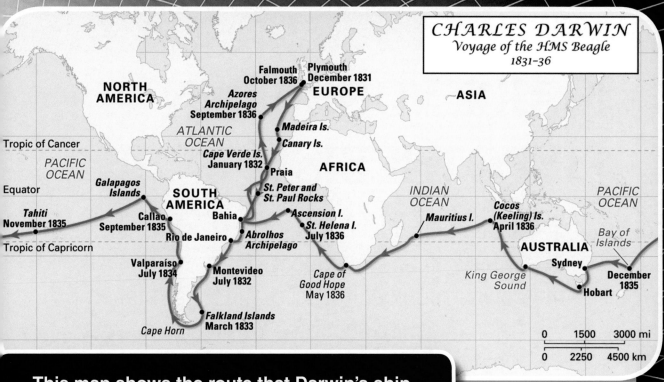

This map shows the route that Darwin's ship, the HMS *Beagle*, took on its five-year journey.

Many other scientists have tested Darwin's ideas and hypotheses. They have confirmed, challenged, and improved Darwin's theory. By doing that they have increased our understanding of how living beings came to be the way they are.

CHAPTER 4

MAKE YOUR OWN HYPOTHESIS

You don't need a laboratory or special equipment to perform an experiment. Anyone can make their own experiment by following these steps:

1. Ask a question about the world around you. What are you curious about? What have you seen or read about that you didn't understand? Do you have a **hunch** about something, and do you want to find out if you're right? Figure out exactly what you want to know.

2. Make a list of what you already know about this

VOCABULARY

A **hunch** is a strong feeling about what will happen.

Simple experiments can be done at home, but it's always a good idea to have an adult help out.

subject, even if it doesn't seem important. It may be useful later.

3. Create a hypothesis and a prediction. Make a

statement about what you think is true, and then create an if/then statement describing what you are going to do to prove your hypothesis.

4. Develop a procedure. List the steps you will take to perform your experiment.
5. Gather materials. Get everything you need for your experiment, and put it in one place.
6. Perform your experiment. Follow your steps, and be sure to record your results.

You can do lots of experiments on your own. For safety, make sure that you talk to an adult about your experiment before you begin.

Writing out your thoughts helps you stay organized. It also may help you discover what information you might be missing.

Experiment #1: Vehicle Ramp

1. **Question:** How does the height of a ramp affect the speed of a toy vehicle?

2. **Background knowledge:** Think about a time you went down a slide or rode your bike down a hill. Did you go faster or slower than you did on a hill that wasn't as steep?

3. **State your hypothesis:** The height of a ramp affects the speed of a vehicle going down it by (choose one):
   a. making it go faster
   b. slowing it down

4. **Now state your prediction:** If the

This toddler has learned through observation that the truck goes quickly down the ramp.

height of a ramp increases, then the speed of the vehicle will (choose one):

    a. increase

    b. decrease

5. **Develop a procedure:** Release a toy car down a ramp at three different heights by placing the ramp on increasingly higher steps on a staircase. Repeat each run three times.

6. **Gather materials:** A long piece of wood or stiff cardboard, toy vehicle, stopwatch or timer.

7. **Perform the experiment:** Follow the steps of your procedure, using the timer to record the times.

8. **Conclusion:** Determine whether your hypothesis was correct.

Experiment #2: Erosion

1. **Question:** Does water volume affect rates of erosion?

COMPARE & CONTRAST

How are experiments you do on your own like ones you do in school? How are they different?

2. **Background knowledge:** Think about playing at the beach, pouring milk in your cereal, or seeing a creek flowing. How does the amount of water change the speed of the flow, or how it moves things out of its way?

3. **State your hypothesis and prediction:** As the volume of water increases, the rate of erosion (choose one):
   a. increases
   b. decreases

Erosion is a process that wears away rock over time. Waves on a beach show this process on a small scale.

If I increase the amount of water I pour into sand, then (choose one):

    a. more sand will be pushed to the sides
    b. less sand will be pushed to the sides

4. **Develop a procedure:** Pour increasing amounts of water onto a pile of sand and measure the width of the path the water makes.
5. **Gather materials:** Shoebox, sand, water, measuring cup, ruler.

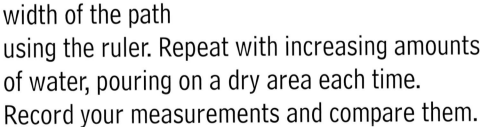

You don't need a laboratory full of equipment to be a scientist. Simple things you can find around your house can be used.

6. **Perform experiment:** Pile the sand up on one side of the box. Pour a small amount of water down the pile, then measure the width of the path using the ruler. Repeat with increasing amounts of water, pouring on a dry area each time. Record your measurements and compare them.

7. **Conclusion:** Was your hypothesis correct?

GLOSSARY

confident Feeling certain that you are correct.

develop To bring to a more advanced state.

dissect To cut a body open to be examined.

erosion The movement of soil and rock from one area of Earth to another through natural causes, such as wind, water, and ice.

evolution The theory that all the kinds of living things that exist today developed from earlier types.

experiment Steps carried out to test a hypothesis.

factor Something that contributes to the result produced.

feces Solid waste that comes from a human or animal.

laboratory A place equipped for doing scientific experiments.

midwife A person trained to help women give birth.

prediction A guess about what will happen in a particular situation.

procedure A method for carrying out a plan.

record To put information in writing.

volume The amount of space something takes up.

FOR MORE INFORMATION

Berne, Emma Carlson. *Guess!: Research and Form a Hypothesis.* New York, NY: PowerKids Press, 2015.

Carmichael, L.E. *Scientific Method in the Real World.* Minneapolis, MN: Core Library, 2013.

Cobb, Vicki. *We Dare You!: Hundreds of Fun Science Experiments You Can Do at Home.* New York, NY: Sky Pony Press, 2015.

Larson, Kristen. *Using the Scientific Method.* Vero Beach, FL: Rourke Publishing, 2014.

Sharkawy, Azza. *Predict It!* (Science Sleuths). New York, NY: Crabtree Publishing Company, 2015.

Yomtov, Nelson. *How to Write a Lab Report.* Ann Arbor, MI: Cherry Lake Publishing, 2014.

WEBSITES

Biology4Kids
http://www.biology4kids.com/files/studies_scimethod.html

PBS Kids
http://pbskids.org/video/ready-jet-go/2365644213

Science Buddies
https://www.sciencebuddies.org/science-fair-projects/science-fair/steps-of-the-scientific-method

Facebook, Twitter: @ScienceBuddies

INDEX